Even Mo
Legends of the Elders

by

John W. Friesen Ph.D., D.Min., D.R.S.

and

Virginia Lyons Friesen Ph.D.

P.A.L.S.- Project Adult Literacy Society
41, 9912 - 106 Street
Edmonton AB T5K 1C5

Illustrations by David J Friesen B. Ed.

DETSELIG
ENTERPRISES LTD

Even More Legends of the Elders

© 2005 John W. Friesen and Virginia Lyons Friesen

Library and Archives Canada Cataloguing in Publication

Freisen, John. W.

   Even more legends of the elders / John W. Friesen and Virginia Lyons Friesen.
ISBN 1-55059-280-7

1. Indians of North America–Folklore. 2.Legends–North America. I.Friesen, Virginia Agnes Lyons, date. II. Title.

E98.F6F738 2005   398.2'089'97   C2004-907425-3

We acknowledge the support of the Government of Canada through the Book Publishing Industry Development Program (BPIDP) for our publishing program.

We also acknowledge the support of the Alberta Foundation for the Arts for our publishing program.

COMMITTED TO THE DEVELOPMENT OF CULTURE AND THE ARTS

SAN 113-0234
ISBN 1-55059-280-7
Printed in Canada

Detselig Enterprises Ltd.
210 - 1220 Kensington Rd NW
Calgary, Alberta T2N 3P5

Telephone: 403-283-0900
Fax: 403-283-6947
Email: temeron@telusplanet.net
www.temerondetselig.com

DETSELIG
ENTERPRISES LTD

Cover design by Alvin Choong

Table of Contents

To the Memory of the late
Marlene Steinhauer,
Cree First Nation
Saddle Lake, Alberta

The Significance of Indian Legends

Legends have sometimes been identified as one of the most common means of transmitting First Nations cultural values and beliefs. There was a time when all cultures relied solely on the oral tradition and there were no written forms of communication. Legends or stories shared between families and communities conveyed important belief systems, ceremonial rituals, and cultural symbols. Aboriginal bands specialized in the use of this medium.

This generation is very fortunate in being able to access Native legends. Appreciation for the preservation of these tales must be extended to several sectors, particularly elders who took upon themselves the responsibility of maintaining the essence of the oral tradition during times when their people were under siege to abandon traditional ways. These guardians of revered knowledge have been successful in keeping many of their valued beliefs and practices alive through very turbulent times. Adherents to the written word who first came into contact with Indigenous cultures, such as traders, missionaries, and anthropologists also rendered a valuable service by committing to writing many stories they learned from their new found acquaintances.

Native legends have a unique identity. They are truly Indigenous stories, and as such they constitute the oral literature of each particular tribal cultural configuration. Indian stories are pictures of Aboriginal life verbally drawn by Indigenous storytellers, showing life from their point of view. Legends deal with spirituality, the origins of things, and various kinds of individual behavior. Legends are often entertaining and they may convey a vast range of cultural knowledge including folkways, values and beliefs. Legends often outline the very basis of a particular cultural pattern. The sacred number four occurs in several of the legends in this volume.

The study of Native legends can be a very rich source of learning. Traditionally, legends appear to have been told for a variety of purposes, both formal and informal. Formal storytelling was usually connected to the occasion of deliberate moral or spiritual instruction. In fact, some legends were considered so sacred or special that their telling was restricted to the celebration of a very special event such as the Sundance. Others were told only during specific seasons. On these occasions, only recognized or designated persons could engage in their telling. Nearly anyone could engage in informal storytelling, and such legends were usually related for their entertainment or instructional value.

It is possible to classify Indian legends into four categories (with some degree of overlap), each of which has a special purpose. The four types of legends are as follows.

(i) **Entertainment legends** are often about the trickster, who is called by different names among the various tribes. For example, the Blackfoot call him Napi, the Crees call him Wisakedjak, the Ojibway call him Nanabush, the Sioux call him îktômni, and other tribes have different names for him like Coyote, Tarantula, or Raven. Stories about the trickster are principally fictional and can be invented and amended even during the process of storytelling.

Trickster stories often involve playing tricks. Sometimes the trickster plays tricks on others and sometimes they play tricks on him. The trickster appears to have the advantage on his unsuspecting audience, however, since he possesses supernatural powers, which he deploys on a whim to startle or to shock. He has powers to raise animals to life and he himself may even die and in four days come to life again. Aside from being amusing, trickster stories often incorporate knowledge about aspects of Aboriginal culture, buffalo hunts, natural phenomena, or rituals, or the relationship between people and animals. In this sense trickster stories can also be instructional.

(ii) **Instructional** or **Explanatory legends** are basically told for the purpose of sharing information about a tribe's culture, history, or origin. These stories explain things. They often use animal motifs to explain why things are the way they are. A child may enquire about the origin of the seasons or the creation of the world and a tale about animal life may be told. For example, a child may ask, "Where did our people come from?" or "Why are crows' feathers black?" Stories told in response to these questions could include adventures of the trickster.

(iii) **Moral legends** are intended to teach ideal or "right" forms of behavior, and are employed to suggest to the listener that a change in attitude or action would be desirable. Since traditional Indian tribes rarely corporally punished their children they sometimes found it useful to hint at the inappropriateness of certain behavior by telling stories. For example, the story might be about an animal that engages in inappropriate behavior and the child is expected to realize that a possible modification of his or her own behavior is the object of the telling.

(iv) **Sacred** or **Spiritual legends** can be told only by a recognized elder or other tribal-approved individual and their telling is considered a form of worship. That tradition is respected in this volume so there are no sacred legends included.

In traditional times, spiritually significant stories were neither told to just anyone who asked nor told by just anyone. In some tribes, sacred legends were considered property and thus their transmission from generation to generation was carefully safeguarded. Selected individuals learned a legend by careful listening; then, on mastering the story, passed it on to succeeding generations, perhaps changing aspects of the story to suit their own tastes. The amendments would center on a different choice of animals or sites referred to in the story and preferred by the teller.

Legends comprised only a part of a tribe's spiritual structure, which also included ceremonies, rituals, songs, and dances. Physical objects such as fetishes, pipes, painted teepee designs, medicine bundles, and shrines of sorts, supplemented these. Familiarity with these components comprised sacred knowledge, and everything learned was committed to memory. Viewed together, these entries represented spiritual connections between people and the universe which, with appropriate care, resulted in a lifestyle of assured food supply, physical well-being and satisfying the needs and wants of the society and its members.

The stories contained in this volume have been drawn from several different sources including fieldwork, personal contact, classroom exchanges, literature, and anthropological studies. Through the years we have visited most of the tribes represented in this book, and have taught university courses in First Nations communities including Blackfoot, Chipewyan, Cree, Stoney (Nakoda Sioux), and Tsuu T'ina (Sarcee). This, the fourth and final volume in this series, is unique because approximately half of these legends originate with Indians in the United States. For more information on stories in this volume, please refer to the teacher's handbook which is available separately.

The essence of each story contained in this volume has been preserved although the legends have been shortened and written in language that may readily be understood by and shared with children. This collection is dedicated to the reality that one cannot value too highly the importance of Indian legends. Through this means, students of Aboriginal ways can learn a great deal about Indian philosophy and, hopefully, increase respect for their ways.

Historical Legends

The Day Spider Brought Light
A Cherokee Legend

When the earth was first formed some people lived on it, without light. Everyone in that part of the world stumbled around in the dark trying to find food and a place to live.

"We need light," said the people. "We can't see what we are doing. We stumble around and bump into things. It is very inconvenient not to have light." The people and the animals decided to have a council and determine what could be done about it.

At the council meeting Fox mentioned that he had heard about people on the other side of the earth who had light. It made all the difference in the world. He also heard that the people with light did not want to share the light. They wanted to keep it to themselves.

Possum offered to help. "I have a wide bushy tail," he said. "I will travel to the village with light and take some. I can hide the light inside my tail and no one will know I have it." Everyone thought this was a good idea, so Possum took off on his adventure.

Possum traveled to the other side of the earth and found the sun hanging on a tree branch. Possum took a small bit of the sun and hid it under his tail. He had not figured that even a bit of the sun could be so hot, but it was. It burned all the fur off his tail and his tail turned bald. Ever since then Possums' tails have been bald.

The people with light found out that Possum had taken a bit of light so they took it back.

Now it was Buzzard's turn. "Let me get some light," he said. "I will not hide the light in my tail. I will put it on the top of my head."

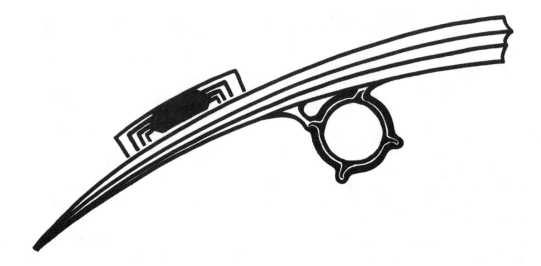

Buzzard flew to the other side of the earth and took the sun in his sharp claws. He put the sun on the top of his head but it burned all the feathers off his head. Buzzard was forced to drop the sun and fly away. Since then, Buzzard's head has been bald.

The people were very sad. There was still no light, and no one had a solution. At last, Spider spoke up. "Let me try to get light." No one believed that Spider could get the light. After all, Spider was so small.

It turned out that the people were wrong. Spider spun a long web from one side of the earth to the other. She also made a small clay pot. No one noticed Spider's work because the web she spun was hard to see. When Spider reached the sun she took a bit of it and put it into the pot. She hurried back home along the web she had spun and gave the light to the people. The people used the light to make fire and cook their food.

Everyone was very grateful to Spider.

The Day Fox Brought Fire
An Apache Legend

Before people came into the world, all the animals and other living things lived in harmony. Fireflies were the only ones who had the secret of fire but they did not want to share it with the other living things. The fireflies guarded their fire with great care and tried to stop anyone who wanted to borrow it. When winter came and the weather grew cold, many of the animals were cold. They huddled together to keep warm and wished they had fire to warm them.

One night the fireflies decided to hold a council meeting to decide on their future. They built a huge fire to warm themselves and posted guards to make sure that no one came near their meeting place. After all, visitors might want to steal their fire. They did not know that Fox had heard about the meeting and hidden himself in the bushes near their fire pit, which was located on a hill. When a live coal fell out of the fire pit and rolled down the hill, Fox grabbed it and ran off with it.

The fireflies saw Fox grab the coal and everyone sprang to their feet and flew off to catch him. Fox is a very wily creature, however, and he managed to dodge the fireflies every time they came near him. Fox ran into the thick forest where he was quite at home and he confused the fireflies who found it difficult to fly very fast in the forest.

As he traveled along, Fox ignited small fires along the way. He lit grasses and bushes and shared the fire with everyone along the way. This made it impossible for the fireflies to stop him. Finally, the fireflies were out of breath and stopped pursuing Fox. They gathered together to discuss the situation. However, one firefly was more persistent and kept on chasing Fox. Finally he flew back to the group and explained what he had seen. Fox had shared fire with everyone along his path. There was no stopping him.

Now every living creature was warm and they were very grateful to Fox.

The Day the Red-Tailed Hawk Brought Fire

A Cowichan Legend

In the old days the Cowichan people lived without fire. They could not cook their food and their homes were sometimes quite cold in the wintertime. They wished for warmth but had no idea how to get it.

One day a group of people were having supper when a beautiful bird with a bright red tail fluttered over their heads. Everyone noticed the bird's bright red tail. This was the red-tailed hawk.

"Do you see this red flame on my tail?" said the visitor. "It is called fire. It is my gift to you."

"What is fire?" everyone asked. "Why do we want fire?"

"Gather up some small pieces of light wood," said the red-tailed hawk. "Then follow me. I will show you what fire can do. Whoever keeps up with me can learn about fire."

The hawk began to fly away and everyone grabbed a piece of light wood and ran after it. The people were very excited to learn about the mystery of fire.

The hawk flew quickly and the people had great difficulty keeping up with it. They ran through brush, over stumps, and through swamps. Still the bird flew on. Most of the people could not keep up and stopped running after the bird. Finally, there were only four people left pursuing the bird. There were two men and two women still chasing the bird.

Suddenly the hawk stopped flying and settled on a low branch. "Come and touch my tail," said the bird. "Feel how warm it is. It will cook your meat and fish and warm your homes. One of you can have it to take back to your village."

"Give it to me," said the first man. "I have kept up with you running through the brush, and swamp, and forest. I deserve it."

"No," said the hawk. "You are a selfish man and would not share the fire with others. You do not deserve it."

"Let me have it," said the second man. "I can make good use of fire. I will do many things with it."

"No," said the hawk. "You are too eager and excited. You might start a huge fire and burn down the forest. You cannot have it."

Then a third person, a woman, spoke up. "Give me the fire and I will only share it with the other women in my village. Then we will be able to cook food for our children."

"No, " said the hawk. "The fire is for everyone. It is for men and women and children. It should be shared with everyone in all the villages. It should not be kept from anyone."

Then the hawk spoke to a fourth person. This woman had barely kept up with the bird in flight.

"Bring your wood to me," said the hawk. "You can have the fire."

"Oh no," said the woman. "I have done nothing to deserve it. One of the others should have it."

"Take the fire," said the red-tailed hawk. "You are always doing good and I know you will share the fire with everyone."

So the woman put her wood to the hawk's bright red tail and the wood began to burn. It gave of a soft warm glow.

Quickly the woman made her way back to the village and shared the fire with her friends and neighbors. The people began to cook their food with fire and use it to warm their homes. Everyone was very happy to have fire.

That is how, long ago, the Cowichan people got fire.

The Day the Buffalo Came
An Apache Legend

When the earth was first created, a powerful chief named Mountain Man owned all the buffalo. He lived on a high mountain with his son, Little Mountain. Mountain Man kept the buffalo carefully corralled so no one could steal them. He would not share a single buffalo with anyone. He would not sell them, trade them, or give them away. All the people wanted to have buffalo for food, shelter, and clothing, but Mountain Man would not give them up.

One day Coyote, the trickster, decided it was time for Mountain Man to share some of his buffalo. He and a group of Apache warriors made a camp near Mountain Man's ranch. During the night they made a careful inspection of the corral where Mountain Man kept the buffalo. As it turned out, the buffalo were housed in a corral made of stone walls. The only entrance was through a door in Mountain Man's house. The situation looked hopeless.

After four days of trying to find ways to get the buffalo, Coyote called a council of the people. The trickster shared with the people the difficult situation they were in. Everyone tried to think of a way to get the buffalo. After hours of discussion, no one could come up with a plan. There was just no way to get into Mountain Man's house.

Finally the trickster spoke. "I have a plan," he said. "Has anyone noticed that Mountain Man's son does not have a pet? He has no one to play with, and no pet for company." Everyone nodded. It was true; Mountain Man's son did not have a pet. Still, no one knew what this had to do with obtaining buffalo. The people knew Coyote was a tricky fellow, so they listened further to his scheme.

Coyote was equal to the occasion. "Listen to this plan," he said. "In the morning, when Little Mountain goes to the brook for water he will see a bird with a broken wing. I will change myself into a bird and pre-

tend I have a broken wing. When Little Mountain sees the bird with the broken wing he will feel sorry for it and take it into the house. Once I am in the house I will release the buffalo."

Everyone liked the trickster's plan and it was put into practice the very next day. But the plan did not work. When Mountain man saw the bird that his son had brought into the house he was very annoyed. "What good is a wounded bird?" he asked his son. "Take it out of the house and release it. It is of no use to us." Sorrowfully, the boy did as his father asked and Coyote, who was disguised as the bird, was taken out of the house.

The next day Coyote tried again. This time he changed himself into a dog. He was sure that Little Mountain would want a dog for a pet. The plan worked, but when Little Mountain took the dog into the house his father scolded him. "Take this dog out of here," he roared. "Put him in the corral with the buffalo." This is exactly what Coyote wanted. He waited until Mountain Man was asleep and then began to bark as loudly as he could. The buffalo were very frightened because they had never heard a dog bark before. They began to run toward the door of the house. The noise of the stampeding buffalo awakened Mountain Man but he could not stop the buffalo. They pushed Mountain Man aside and stormed out of the corral and through the house. Soon they were running loose all over the earth.

Little Mountain started to look for his pet dog but his father stopped him. "That was no dog," he said. "It was Coyote the trickster. He has played a trick on us. We have lost the buffalo."

This is the way the Apache nation finally got the buffalo.

How Corn Came to the People
A Chippewa Legend

Once there was a man and a woman who had four sons. The family lived in the woodlands of Ontario. The man was a hunter but his family was poor and game was scarce. Sometimes the family had very little to eat.

When the oldest son, Black Hawk, reached his teen years it was time for him to go on a vision quest. His father took him to a lodge far away from the village and told him to remain there for four days and four nights. Black Hawk would eat no food during this time and he would pray to the Creator for a special dream. Perhaps an animal or bird spirit would visit him and give him a special message. That message would give him guidance for the rest of his life.

Black Hawk remained in the lodge as his father had instructed him and began to pray. At the end of the day when he was lying down, a strange visitor entered into the lodge. The visitor wore green and white clothing and had a bright plume of feathers on his head.

"Get up, young fellow," said the visitor. "The Creator has sent me to give you a special test. I want you to get up and wrestle with me. I want to see how strong you are."

Black Hawk was a bit weak because he had not eaten all day but he began to wrestle with the visitor. The visitor was very strong and soon it looked as though Black Hawk would lose. Suddenly, the visitor vanished.

At the end of the second day the visitor returned and Black Hawk wrestled with him again. Now Black Hawk was even weaker for lack of food but he did as the visitor requested. Again the visitor disappeared. The same thing happened on the third day.

At dawn on the fourth day Black Hawk's father arrived to see his son and ask him if he had received a vision.

"No, father, I did not receive a special dream," said Black Hawk, and he told his father about the strange visitor.

"I have one more day left," said Black Hawk. "I am sure something will happen. Perhaps we will find out who the visitor is."

Black Hawk's father agreed, and although he was very weak by now, Black Hawk spent the fourth day in prayer. Sure enough, at the end of the day, the visitor returned.

"Wrestle with me," he coaxed Black Hawk. "You have shown yourself to be very brave. Let us see how strong you still are."

By now the weakened Black Hawk could hardly wrestle, but he did his best and wrestled hard. When he was all tired out, the visitor let him lie down and spoke to him.

"You have been tested and I have found you worthy," he said. "I have a gift for you. It is a gift for your people. When I go away, I will leave you my clothes and plume. You are to put them into the ground and cover them with soil. Put fresh dirt on them every week and water them. Soon you will have a special gift for the people of your village."

The next day when his father returned Black Hawk told him about his unusual experience. Together they planted the visitor's clothes and plume. They watered the ground and kept it free of weeds.

Some time went by and then little green and white shoots appeared in the planted ground. After a few weeks the shoots grew into tall corn stalks and ears with seeds appeared on them. Black Hawk told his father that the grown ears could be roasted and provide food for the people. He told his father everything that the visitor had said.

Soon the corn was ripe and the people picked the ears of corn and roasted them. Everyone joined in the first corn feast.

That is how corn came to the Chippewa people and soon people in other parts of the world began to enjoy it as well.

It all happened because a determined young boy named Black Hawk had a very special vision.

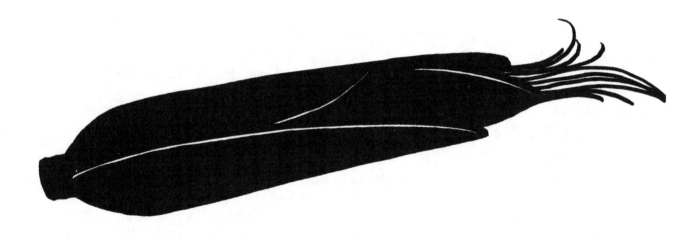

How Corn Came to the People
An Ottawa Legend

The Ottawa Indians have lived in eastern Canada for a long, long time. They used to hunt small animals, fish the rivers, and harvest wild rice for food. One day they received the magic gift of corn.

It happened that Manitoulin Island where they lived was guarded by a medicine man named Good Spirit. He had strong powers. Everyone in the tribe respected Good Spirit and often went to him for advice.

One day Good Spirit happened to be walking in the woods when a stranger approached him. The stranger was not very tall and he wore a hat with red feathers on it.

"Hello there, Good Spirit," said the stranger. "I understand you are a strong man. My name is Corn Man. Come and sit with me and we will smoke the pipe together. Then we will have a wrestling match to see who is stronger."

Good Spirit smiled, for the stranger was a rather small man and he certainly did not look very strong. Good Spirit sat down with Corn Man and they smoked the pipe together. Good Spirit wondered about the meaning of Corn Man's name.

After the two had smoked together for a while, Corn Man said it was time for them to wrestle. Good Spirit agreed but he was afraid he might hurt the little man. However, once they started wrestling, it was a different story. Good Spirit found that Corn Man was very strong and he had to fight with all his might. Finally, Good Spirit felt Corn Man growing weaker and he tripped Corn Man and threw him to the ground.

"I have won," cried Good Spirit, and Corn man agreed. "Now that you have won, I will give you a gift," said Corn Man. "You surely are the winner."

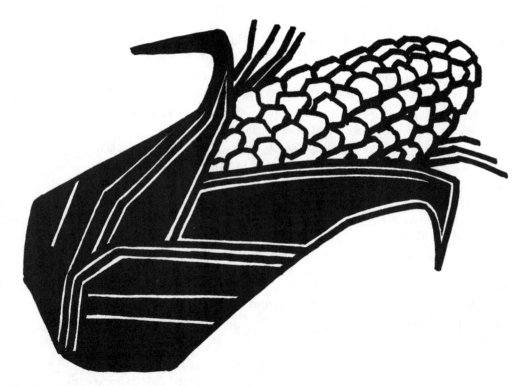

"Pick me up," said Corn Man. "Pull off my outer shell and break the inner cob in three pieces. Then plant the three pieces of cob in the ground near the trees. Then after one moon has passed, come back and observe the place where you planted the cobs."

Good Spirit did as he was told and sure enough, when he returned one moon later to the planting ground he saw three green blades coming out of the ground. All summer he watched as the stalks grew taller. To his surprise, in the fall he saw beautiful ears of corn on the stalks. Suddenly a voice spoke to him.

"You have grown the corn, Good Spirit. Now boil the corn and feed it to your people." It was the voice of Corn Man.

It was his gift to Good Spirit. It was his gift to the Ottawa Indians.

The First Meeting
A Cheyenne Legend

The Cheyenne were once a proud people of the plains. They were great hunters and were feared by many of their neighbors. They hunted buffalo and ruled a vast area of the southern plains, but this was all to change.

One summer day when the Cheyenne were camped alongside a river, a man named Big Eagle and his wife saw a tall thin man come toward their teepee. He looked tired and hungry, and although he looked like one of the Cheyenne people, his skin was much whiter. Big Eagle and his wife invited the man into their home and gave him something to eat. Soon afterward he fell asleep. Big Eagle and his wife decided to keep the visitor's presence a secret from the rest of the people. They wanted to see what would happen.

Several days passed and the chiefs announced that the village would be moving. Big Eagle knew that this would make it difficult to keep the stranger's presence a secret so he decided to share the information with village leaders. "This man is my brother," Big Eagle told the chiefs. "When the village is relocated, he will come with us. He is one of us now." Big Eagle was a much respected man in the village so the chiefs agreed.

As time went on the stranger regained his strength and thanked Big Eagle for his help. He learned sign language and was able to speak a few words in Cheyenne. He began to share information about the world from which he came. "We have many good things to trade with you," he told Big Eagle. You must learn about our world and we will learn about yours. We have knives, steel needles, and cooking pots to share with you. You can teach us how to live in this land."

The stranger went on to tell Big Eagle about guns that used black powder and sent hard pieces of metal toward wild game. He said that the guns were much more effective than bows and arrows. Big Eagle believed the stranger and said he would like to learn more about these new things.

He and his friends gave the stranger many furs as gifts and the man returned east, back to the land he came from.

Many moons passed and finally the stranger returned. Big Eagle recognized him right away. The man had brought gifts of knives, needles, and pots of steel. He showed Big Eagle how to use them. He also brought guns with him. Big Eagle was grateful for the gifts.

This is how the Europeans first met the Cheyenne.

The First Meeting
An Ojibway Legend

Once there lived among the Ojibway people of Lake Superior a medicine man who could tell what would happen in the future. He was a prophet and would often have strange dreams. Sometimes he went off by himself to fast, take sweatbaths, and pray. Then he would come back into the village and speak to the people.

One day the prophet told of newcomers with white skin who would arrive in the land from across the Big Water. He said they would have tall canoes and very sharp knives. They would point long black sticks at animals, and the sticks would make loud noises and kill the animals. Then the newcomers would take the animals' furs.

The people listened as the prophet told his story. It took him nearly half a day to describe the way the visitors would look and what they wanted. He said that they would arrive from across the Big Water.

When the people heard about the newcomers they decided to prepare to meet them. They prepared many canoes and traveled to the Big Water where they heard the newcomers would be arriving. It took many days and nights to arrive at the Big Water, but the newcomers finally arrived. The Ojibway made camp in a large clearing, put up their wigwams, and waited for their guests to appear.

The Ojibway discovered that many trees had been cut down in the clearing, leaving only stumps. The Ojibway thought that large beavers with huge teeth must have cut them down. They had never seen beavers that large anywhere.

"Oh no," said their prophet. "These trees were cut down with the large knives that the visitors have."

The people were filled with wonder and fear. What kind of people were these anyway? They were soon to find out.

When the Europeans met the Ojibway they brought gifts of brightly-colored fabric and pieces of wood with tools of steel attached to them. The tools were rakes and shovels and hoes to plant gardens.

The Ojibway were delighted with the gifts and hurried home to tell their friends about their first meeting with the white men from Europe.

The Day the Horses Came
A Comanche Legend

Before the Europeans came to North America the Indian people did not have horses. Instead, when they wanted to travel somewhere they walked and used dogs to pull their belongings on a travois. A travois is made up of two long rails tied to the dog's body and the dog pulls them. The two rails are placed wider apart at the dog's back with a hide drawn across them behind the dog. Possessions are placed on the hide and the dog carries the load by dragging the poles along the ground.

One day long ago, four visitors arrived in the Comanche camp with a dozen huge animals that looked like large dogs. The animals had long tails and hair grew all along their long necks. They dragged long travois behind them loaded with great piles of goods. Three of the visitors sat on the large animals. The Comanches thought the strange animals looked like they might be magic dogs, but they were really horses.

The village dogs barked at the horses and the women and children were so frightened that they scurried into their teepees. The warriors and hunters stared at the visitors with their mouths open.

"These men might be traders," said one of the hunters. "Let us see what they want."

The visitors used sign language to indicate that they wanted to trade the horses for furs and food. One of them rubbed his stomach and a woman exclaimed in the Comanche language, "I think he wants something to eat." She placed a plate of meat before the man and he passed it among his friends. Everyone had something to eat.

One of the visitors pointed at some furs and then to his horse. A warrior knew just what the man wanted. He began to pile up furs until the visitor raised his arms and called, "Stop." This meant that the pile of furs would be traded for one horse. Using sign language the two parties traded several horses for Comanche goods.

Before long other hunters and warriors came forward and offered to trade for a horse. Using sign language the visitors and the Indians made many trades. Soon the Comanches began to raise horses of their own and trade them with other tribes.

This is how horses came to the Comanche people. Before many years passed they became the finest horsemen on the plains.

The Day the Horses Came
A Peigan Legend

The Peigan First Nation is a member of the Blackfoot Confederacy. One night a Peigan warrior named Red Gun had a dream. In the dream a voice told Red Gun to go to a nearby lake where he would see some unusual animals. He was to take a rope and tie it around the animals' necks and lead them home. These strange animals could be used to pull travois and carry large packs. They would be a great help to the Peigan Indians.

When Red Gun awoke, he did as he was told in the dream. He took a long rope made of strips of rawhide and travelled a long distance to the lake he had seen in his dream. He dug a pit large enough to hide in and waited. Soon he saw all kinds of animals come to drink from the lake. There were deer, antelope, coyotes, wolves, and buffalo. They were all thirsty.

Red Gun waited. Surely these were not the animals described in his dream. At last a herd of unusual animals came. They were as large as elks, and very sleek looking. They had long manes and their tails hung to the ground. They were also fast runners. Some of them came running to the edge of the lake and Red Gun could see that they had great speed.

The same voice that Red Gun heard in his dream now whispered in his ear, "Throw your rope and catch one of them." Quickly Red Gun threw his rope and it landed around the neck of a tall stallion. The horse struggled to get away from the rope but Red Gun hung on tight. After a fierce fight the horse won and ran off with the rope. Then the whole herd of horses disappeared into the forest and Red Gun lost sight of them.

Feeling like a failure, Red Gun returned to his village. He told an elder about his vision and the elder told him to be patient. That night Red Gun dreamed his dream again. The voice in the dream told him, "You will have four chances to catch the horses. If you fail after four tries you will never see horses again." Red Gun woke with a start.

The next day Red Gun returned to the lake determined to catch a horse. Again he hid in the pit he had dug and waited. Soon the various animals came to drink, including the horses. Carefully Red Gun swung his rope and caught one of the younger, smaller horses. It struggled to be free, but Red Gun tied his rope to a tree and the animal could not escape. Red Gun caught several more horses and then brought them into the Peigan village. The people were frightened of the horses since they had never seen horses before. Gradually the people got used to them, especially after Red Gun told them how useful horses could be. Soon the people used the horses to pull travois and carry large packs. The Peigans called the horses Elk Dogs.

This is how the Peigan people first got horses.

Explanatory Legends

The First Rainbow
A Stoney Legend

Long ago there was a great Stoney hunter named Big Stone who provided his family and his neighbors with plenty of food. Big Stone obtained much game with his trusty bow and arrows but he was never satisfied. He always wanted to hunt more game.

One day Big Stone had an idea. Why not make a bigger bow and longer arrows so he could hunt even bigger game? Big Stone looked to the sky and saw the rainbow. He decided that the rainbow would make a great bow because it was so colorful. The more he looked at the rainbow the more he knew he had to have it.

Big Stone climbed a tall tree on the highest mountain he could find. Then he reached toward the rainbow and grabbed it with his hands. As he grabbed it, the colors disappeared. Angrily Big Stone threw the rainbow into a lake nearby. The rainbow broke into many small pieces and rolled down into the water. The beautiful colors spread throughout the water at the bottom of the lake. Today they may be seen in Lake Louise, Alberta, during the morning right after sunrise.

The Creator soon put another rainbow into the sky and today we can see it after every rain.

The Origin of Strawberries
A Cherokee Legend

When the first man and woman were created they were very happy. They lived in a beautiful garden with plenty of fruits and vegetables for food. There were animals and birds in the garden and the man and woman were friends with them. Then things changed.

One day the man and woman had an argument. The woman got so angry with her husband that she left their wigwam and went for a long walk. Her husband followed her and tried to talk to her but the woman would not listen.

As the woman walked along she should have seen the beautiful things she passed, but she did not notice them. There were bushes of many kinds, pretty flowers, and even berries to eat. Still, the woman would not stop. She was too angry to see anything. Her husband followed her, although he was getting further and further behind.

The Creator looked down from the sky and saw what was going on. He felt sorry for the man and decided to do something about it. Quickly the Creator made some beautiful red berries and put them on the ground right in front of the woman. When she saw the berries, the woman stopped and took a close look at them. They looked good enough to eat so she put one in her mouth and tasted it. It tasted very sweet. She picked another one and ate it. It was delicious.

Quickly she looked around to see if there was someone with whom she could share the berries. There was no one nearby. Then she thought about her husband and decided to wait for him. In her excitement she forgot about her anger. She was too excited about sharing her new discovery. When her husband arrived she gave him some of the berries and the two of them chatted happily. They were no longer angry with one another.

Today, we call the red berries, strawberries. As you may sometime discover, it is difficult to eat strawberries and be angry at anyone.

The Origin of Butterflies
A Papago Legend

A group of children was playing games in the village and the Creator was watching them. He noticed how happy they were. They laughed and sang as they played.

"One day these children will grow old and weak," the Creator noted. "Their skin will become wrinkled, their hair will turn grey, and their teeth will fall out. It will be a sad day. Even the leaves of the trees will turn color and die. Soon there will be nothing left of them. This is the way of all life."

The Creator grew sad as He watched these things come to pass. He probably could have changed the way things are, but they had been that way for a long, long time. He decided to leave things that way.

As the Creator looked around for something to cheer Him up, he noticed the various beautiful colors in the universe. The sky was clear blue, the trees were green, and the falling leaves were red, orange, brown, and yellow. The birds sang lots of different songs, as many songs as flowers have colors. The Creator smiled. Now here was something to cheer Him up.

The Creator visited the children in the village and gave them a great big bag. "Take this," He said. "Open it up. What is inside will make you happy."

The children opened the bag and at once hundreds of beautiful butterflies flew into the air, settling on the children's heads, then fluttering up to sip the nectar from nearby flowers." The butterflies began to sing and the children laughed with delight. They had never seen nor heard anything so beautiful.

A group of songbirds came to the Creator and said, "Why did you give a song to the butterflies and to us as well? Did you not give one gift to each creature? You gave us a song and the butterflies their beauty."

"You are right," the Creator told the songbirds. "You must keep your songs and the butterflies must keep their beauty." Ever since then butterflies have remained beautifully colorful but silent, and songbirds have kept their songs.

The Origin of Thunderbird
A Haida Legend

The Haida people are famous for their carved totem poles. They use a variety of figures on their totem poles including the whale, bear, wolf, eagle, frog, kingfisher, and raven. Often the thunderbird will be seen at the top of their totem poles. There would probably not be a thunderbird on any totem pole if it were not for the events described here.

There was once a young Haida boy named Bent Foot who was often teased because his foot was bent out of shape. Bent Foot could not run like other boys so he was often left out of the games they played. He spent a lot of his time watching the village carver make totem poles. Someday he hoped to become a village carver as well.

Bent Foot's friends sometimes teased him about wanting to become a carver. "You might want to grow up first," they told him. "Only men can carve totem poles and you are a bit too young. Why don't you try to carve a picture of thunder first. No one has ever done that." The teasing did not deter Bent Foot. He knew what he wanted to do with his life.

Bent Foot continued to watch the village carvers. He watched every move they made, often imitating it with his hands as he watched. He often asked the carvers to let him help with carving but they only laughed at him. "Why don't you go and carve Thunder," they teased. "No one has ever done that." Then they went on with their carving. Bent Foot decided to do just that.

Bent Foot got into his canoe and followed Thunder. Every time there was a loud clap of thunder he would paddle after it. He wanted to talk with Thunder, but Thunder never seemed to stay still very long. Always Thunder seemed to be just around the corner and Bent Foot could never catch him.

The water grew rough, but Bent Foot was not frightened. He had a mission and he was determined to fulfill it. Suddenly he saw the shadow of a huge bird flying across the sky. The bird was followed by the sound of a loud clap of thunder. Bent Foot could hardly believe his eyes. He had found Thunder. Suddenly a loud voice from above spoke to Bent Foot. "Who are you and what do you want," said the voice. Bent Foot looked up and saw Thunderbird above him.

"My name is Bent Foot and I want to be a carver," said Bent Foot. "I came to find Thunder."

"Well, you have found Thunder," said Thunderbird. "If you really want to be a carver I can fly you home now and you can start carving right away. I can promise you that your talent will be recognized. I will do this for you on one condition."

"What is that condition?" asked Bent Foot. "You must carve a thunderbird on the top of every totem pole you carve," said Thunderbird. "If you promise to do that I will take you home and you will become a famous carver."

Bent Foot was delighted. He agreed to do as Thunderbird asked. After all, he had found Thunder so he could not be happier. Quickly he climbed aboard Thunderbird's back and soon found himself in his home village. When he began his work the other carvers immediately recognized his talent. Thunderbird appeared at the very top of Bent Foot's first totem pole.

Bent Foot carved totem poles for many years after that, and he kept his promise. Thunderbird appeared at the top of every pole he carved.

The Origin of Bear Rock
A Sioux Legend

There is an unusually tall rock tower in the State of Wyoming known as Bear Rock. NonNative people call the tower, Devil's Tower, but its Indian name is Bear Rock. Bear Rock tower is 378 metres (1227 feet) high but only one hectare (an acre and a half) in size at the top. The sides of the tower are covered with huge scratch-like marks. The Sioux believe that the scratches were made by a huge grizzly bear. This is the story of Bear Rock.

A long time ago two young Sioux boys were playing in the woods when they suddenly realized they were lost. Neither of them knew the way home. For four days they wandered aimlessly in the woods, and worried that they might never be found. To stay alive they ate berries, dug up wild turnips, and drank water from a creek. They even managed to snare a rabbit and roast it over an open fire.

On the fourth day the boys began to think they were being followed. They heard unusual animal noises and turned around to see what was causing the noises. Suddenly they heard a very loud roar and discovered a great big grizzly bear behind them. Needless to say, the boys took off in a great big hurry. As they ran for their lives, one of the boys stumbled but he got up quickly and continued running. Soon the boys could feel the hot breath of the bear on the back of their necks. It seemed there was no hope.

As they ran the boys prayed to the Creator to save them. Desperately they looked for a place of escape. Suddenly, they spied a high rock ahead of them and scurried to the top of it. They soon realized it was of little use. They realized that bear's long arms could still reach them. Then without warning, the rock upon which the boys were standing began to rise. It rose higher and higher until it felt to the boys as if they had reached the sky. The bear was left at the bottom of this tall tower. Angrily the bear began scratching the sides of the rock tower and the marks left by the bear's claws are still visible today.

After some time the bear gave up his pursuit and left the area. Now the boys wondered how they were going to get down from the tall rock tower. Again they prayed to the Creator and the Creator sent four eagles to the top of the tower. Each boy grabbed onto the feet of two eagles and was safely flown to the ground. As they reached the bottom of the tower they discovered their families waiting for them.

Today you can visit Bear Rock in northeast Wyoming, and touch the scratches that the bear made in the rock.

Why Thrushes Sing So Sweetly

An Iroquois Legend

When the world was created, birds could not sing. They flew around the earth but they did not make a noise. The birds wished they could sing songs, but they were unable.

One day the Creator visited earth to see what He had made. As He walked in the woods among the birds and animals, He noticed that something seemed to be missing. It was too quiet. The Creator listened carefully and He heard the whistle of the wind in the trees, the sound of a bubbling brook, and the crackle of a warm fire. Still, these were not the sounds He wanted to hear.

As the Creator looked around, he noticed that the birds were silent. He called all the birds together for a council. They came from far and near. The eagle came from his lofty place in the sky, and robins and geese and bluebirds came. The tiny sparrow came as well. There were birds everywhere.

"I have decided to give you all a song," said the Creator. "You should all be able to sing. Tomorrow I want you all to fly as high into the sky as you can and you will find a song. Each one of you will have a different song. The one that flies the highest will have the prettiest song."

The little brown thrush was seated beside the great eagle. "How can I compete with this powerful bird," thought Thrush. "Surely Eagle will fly the highest and find the prettiest song." Then Thrush came up with a clever plan. The next day as Eagle prepared to fly high into the sky, Thrush hid himself in the Eagle's feathers. Then with a swish of his mighty wings, Eagle took off and flew high into the sky. Perched among Eagle's feathers, the brown thrush waited.

When Eagle had flown up high and found his song, Thrush took off from among Eagle's feathers. He flew a little higher than Eagle and found the prettiest song of all.

The next day the birds gathered in council to hear one another's songs. When they listened to Thrush's song they knew that he had flown the highest. They also realized that he had cheated because they knew that Thrush could not fly higher than Eagle. Suddenly Thrush felt ashamed. He knew it was not right for him to cheat. Quickly he hid himself away from all the other birds.

Today when you hear Thrush's song you will discover that it is the prettiest song of all the birds. You will also find that Thrush is very shy. This is because he is ashamed that he cheated.

Why Beavers Have Flat Tails

A Paiute Legend

Long ago Beaver had a beautiful bushy tail. He was very proud of his bushy tail and often showed it off to the other creatures in the forest. Sometimes the other animals got a bit annoyed with Beaver because he was always showing off his soft, thick tail. Whenever the wind blew it looked like Beaver's tail had several glowing colors in it.

Beaver's tail was also very useful. Whenever he wanted to take a nap he used his soft, blanket-like tail to lie on. When nights were cold, Beaver covered his back with his beautiful, furry tail. Sometimes his little ones cuddled with their father in his nice bushy tail.

One day the animals decided that they should have fire. No one in the forest had fire and everyone wanted to have it. Fire was warm. It could be used to cook food and warm homes. The animals held a council to see if anyone would volunteer to get fire.

The animals knew about a tribe of people across the mountain who had fire but the people refused to share it. Several animals volunteered to go across the mountain to obtain fire from the people. Every animal who went to get fire was refused. The people always said no. The animals held a council and decided that it was Beaver's turn to try to get fire.

Beaver was not very excited about having been chosen to get fire but he wanted to do his duty. Reluctantly, he crossed the mountain to meet with the fire people. When he got there he strutted his beautiful tail just as he always did back home. This made some people angry, and one of them said, "I am going to cut that fellow's tail off. He need not show off so much."

One of the men took off after Beaver who jumped across a huge fire just to get away. When he did so, his bushy tail caught fire. Now knowing what to do, Beaver ran home as fast as he could. Since his tail was on fire, the forest began to burn wherever he ran. When Beaver got to a river he jumped in, but it was too late. All the hair on his bushy tail was burned off. Now it was completely flat and bald. Beaver was so ashamed that he decided to live in the river after that. This was the cost of bringing fire to his community.

Because of this unfortunate experience, today Beaver still lives in the river. He builds his home in the river, and comes out mostly at night to cut logs or hunt for food. His bare tail is useful as a paddle when he swims and sometimes he slaps it on the water as a warning to his neighbors that someone is coming. He also uses his tail to hold logs in place when he is building his home.

His friends feel sorry for him, but they always remember that it was Beaver who brought fire to the forest.

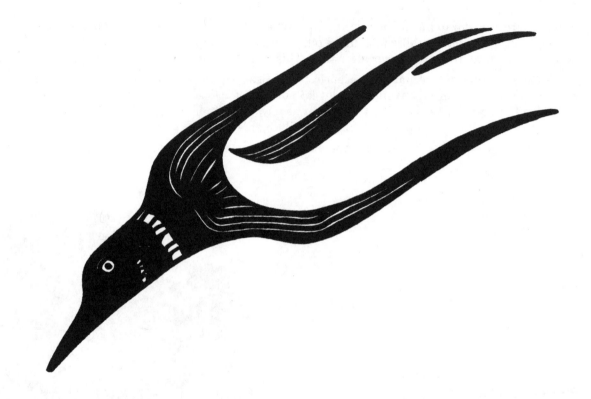

Why Loons are Shallow Divers
A Mi'kmaq Legend

One day Glooscap was traveling to Newfoundland when he saw Loon circling overhead. Glooscap called out to Loon, enquiring as to what the bird was doing.

"I was looking for you," Loon replied. "I want to be your servant." Glooscap then gave Loon an unusual cry and when Loon tried it out he was surprised at the sound.

"What is that sound?" asked Loon. "It sounds like a faraway cry."

Glooscap answered, "That is the way I made the sound. It is your cry, and your cry alone. From now on only loons will make that cry."

When Glooscap arrived in Newfoundland the people were glad to see him so he made each of them a loon. This gave rise to a lot of loon sayings such as, "Loon is calling Glooscap, it is looning to Glooscap," or "Loon is in need of Glooscap."

One day Loon, who loved to dive, dove so deep into the water that he became stuck in the weeds at the bottom of the lake. The people wondered what had happened to him and finally they called on Glooscap to help. Glooscap stood by the lake and listened. Suddenly he heard loud thunder, but he told Thunder to be quiet.

"Be still," he ordered, "I am trying to hear Loon."

"Don't be angry," said Thunder, "I am merely trying to tell you that Loon is stuck at the bottom of the lake." Glooscap dove into the lake, retrieved Loon and declared, "From now on you will dive into the lake but never down to the weeds."

And to this day all loons are shallow divers.

Why Spiders Have Long Legs
A Salish Legend

Long ago Spider was a skilled hunter and warrior. Spider lived with his grandmother and took care of her. There was always plenty of food in their home because Spider was a very good hunter. Spider's skills made him a very desirable mate and many young maidens in the village wanted to marry Spider.

One day Spider came up with a plan to determine which of the young maidens he would marry. He called it the "smoke test." He planned to invite the women to his house, one at a time. He would then fill the house with lots of smoke and see if the maiden would remain in the house. If she stayed in the house it meant that she was very serious about marrying Spider.

One by one the young women came to Spider's house and one by one he gave them the smoke test. As soon as the woman entered the house Spider would close the door of the house, and turn on the smoke. As it happened, one by one the young women failed the test because they went outside the house to get some air. Spider grinned with glee.

Then things changed. Spider met a young woman named Little Deer and he liked her very much. He invited Little Deer into the house but he made only a very light smoke in the house so that she could stand it. He wanted her to pass the smoke test. Spider did not know that Little Deer had heard of his plan and was prepared for it.

On her way over to Spider's house, Little Deer took some medicine that would help her with the smoke. When Spider turned on his smoke test, Little Deer made the smoke strong with her medicine. When Spider began to cough from the strong smoke, Little Deer took one of his legs and pulled it hard until it also grew very long. Little Deer did this with each of Spider's legs and began to laugh. Spider was now a Daddy Long Legs, and ever since then spiders have had long legs.

Suddenly Spider's grandmother came into the house and saw what Little Deer had done. She knew that none of the other village maidens would want to marry Spider any more so she ruled that Little Deer would be Spider's wife. Grandmother's medicine was stronger than Little Deer's so there was nothing Little Deer could do. She had to marry Spider.

Spider loved Little Deer despite what she had done to him. He forgave her and they lived together for a long time.

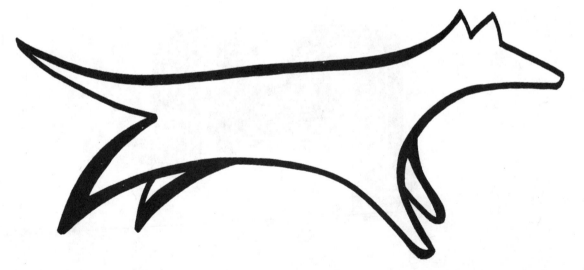

Why Coyotes' Coats are Sand-Colored

A Pima Legend

One day Coyote was unhappy about the color of his coat. He noticed that his friends had beautiful coats, but his was quite dull in color. Bear's coat was black, Wolf's coat was grey, and Fox's was red. Even the birds wore brightly colored coats.

Coyote went to his friend Bluebird and asked for his help. "Look at my shabby coat," he said to Bluebird. "Yours is such a pretty blue. Can you help me get a pretty blue coat like yours?"

"Certainly," said Bluebird. "There is a special lake that I bathe in. It will make your coat blue just like mine."

Coyote was very pleased. He could hardly wait to brighten up his dull coat.

"There are rules to follow if you want to have a coat like mine," said Bluebird. "After you bathe in the lake you must not look at your coat for four days. You also must not look at your shadow either for four days. If you do, your coat will turn into the color of sand. Coyote agreed to obey the rules.

Bluebird took Coyote to the magic lake and Coyote jumped in. He dipped into the water four times but did not look at his coat. As he walked back to the village he thought to himself, "Just wait until my friends see me now. They will all be envious of my new blue coat."

Coyote decided that he would take a quick peek at his shadow just to make sure that the magic lake had worked. Just as he bent his neck to take a quick look at his shadow, Coyote stumbled on a rock and fell headlong into the sand. The sand covered his wet coat and stuck to it. His coat was all sand-colored. Coyote was shocked by what happened.

Quickly he returned to the magic lake. He dipped in the water four times and looked at his coat. It was still the color of sand. He dipped again and again, but alas, the color of his coat did not change. He had disobeyed the rules.

From that day to this, the coats of coyotes have been the color of sand.

About the Authors

John W. Friesen, Ph.D., D.Min., D.R.S., is a Professor in the Graduate Division of Educational Research at the University of Calgary where he teaches courses in Aboriginal history and education. He is an ordained minister with the All Native Circle Conference of the United Church of Canada, the recipient of three eagle feathers, and author of more than 40 books including the following Detselig titles:

Schools With A Purpose, 1983;

The Cultural Maze: Complex Questions on Native Destiny in Western Canada, 1991;

When Cultures Clash: Case Studies in Multiculturalism, 1993;

Pick one: A User-Friendly Guide to Religion, 1995;

Rediscovering the First Nations of Canada, 1997;

Sayings of the Elders: An Anthology of First Nations' Wisdom, 1998;

First Nations of the Plains: Creative, Adaptable and Enduring, 1999;

Aboriginal Spirituality and Biblical Theology: Closer Than You Think, 2000;

Legends of the Elders, 2000;

Aboriginal Education in Canada: A Plea for Integration (co-author), 2002;

Sayings of a Philosopher, 2004;

Still More Legends of the Elders (co-author), 2004; and

We Are Included: The Métis People of Canada Realize Riel's Vision (co-author), 2004.

Virginia Lyons Friesen, Ph.D., is a Sessional Instructor in the Faculty of Communication and Culture at the University of Calgary. An Early Childhood Education Specialist, she holds a Certificate in Counseling from the Institute of Pastoral Counseling in Akron, Ohio. She served as Director of Christian Education with the Morley United Church on the Stoney (Nakoda Sioux) Indian Reserve from 1988 to 2001.

She has presented papers at learned conferences and is co-author of:

Grade Expectations: A Multicultural Handbook for Teachers (Alberta Teachers' Association, 1995);

In Defense of Public Schools in North America (Detselig, 2001);

Aboriginal Education in Canada: A Plea for Integration (Detselig, 2002);

More Legends of the Elders (Detselig, 2004);

The Palgrave Companion to North American Utopias (Palgrave Macmillan, 2004);

Still More Legends of the Elders (Detselig 2004); and

We Are Included: The Métis People of Canada Realize Riel's Vision (Detselig, 2004).